LET'S EXPERIMENT

Optical Illusions

Author Mattia Crivellini
Illustrator Rossella Trionfetti

PowerKiDS press
NEW YORK

CONTENTS

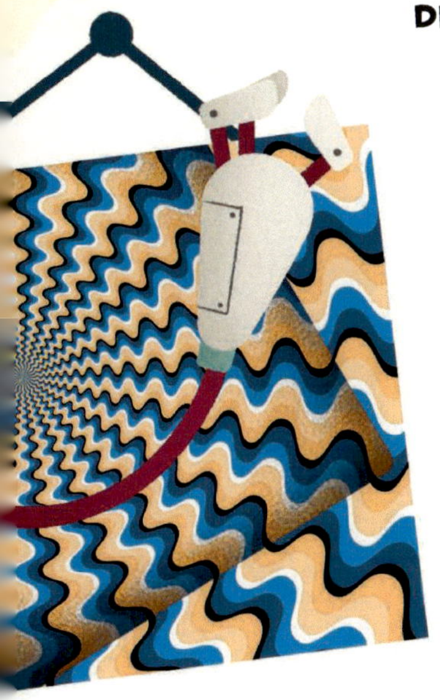

THE SCIENTIFIC METHOD

The **SCIENTIFIC METHOD** is the way in which **SCIENCE** investigates the **REALITY** around us. It is the most reliable method we know to progress in the **KNOWLEDGE** of things and the world.

Scientific does not mean "accurate." Instead, it means something is **reproducible**, that is, that it can be repeated. With the same initial conditions, we expect the experiment to always have the same result. The scientific method is **EXPERIMENTAL**, that is, based on experiments, tests, and observations, and this is the fun part in which the scientist becomes creative!

THE MAIN STAGES OF EXPERIMENTAL SCIENTIFIC METHOD ARE:

1. Observing a phenomenon and asking yourself questions.
2. Formulating a hypothesis, that is, a possible explanation of the phenomenon.
3. Carrying out an experiment to check if the hypothesis is correct.
4. Analyzing the results.
5. Repeating the experiment in different ways.
6. Coming to a conclusion and establishing a rule.

TRAVELING WITH YOU!

I'm **GREG** the **ROBOT**, an advanced form of artificial intelligence. I have a positronic brain with too many mistakes in it.

My name is **BOB**. I love pizza, and I'm a big movie fan. They say I'm a dynamic and very curious guy.

You can call me **PROF. ALBERT**. I'm a renowned scientist and a lover of outdoor trips and cycling. I'm passionate about life, the universe, and...everything!

TWO WORDS: SAFETY FIRST!

1. Before doing any experiment, always read all the instructions carefully.

2. It is forbidden to eat or drink during the experiments and, above all, to eat or drink your experiment! It's a bad idea! Don't do it.

3. Use old clothes because you will get dirty!

4. Wash your hands after every experiment!

5. Always ask an adult before using sharp utensils, stoves, or household appliances.

6. Throw away any garbage or substances in the correct trash can.

Some of the scientific activities in the book require adult supervision.

All the words in CAPITAL LETTERS are in the Glossary on pages 46–47, where the terms are explained in more detail.

OPTICAL ILLUSIONS

An OPTICAL ILLUSION is caused by our VISUAL SYSTEM deceiving us. It makes us perceive something that is not there or that appears to differ from reality.

Scientists classify illusions according to the mechanism that creates them, dividing them into three different categories: **OPTICAL, PERCEPTUAL,** and **COGNITIVE.**

OPTICAL

These are caused by phenomena related to the properties of light and are not dependent on the human eye; for example, mirages in the desert.

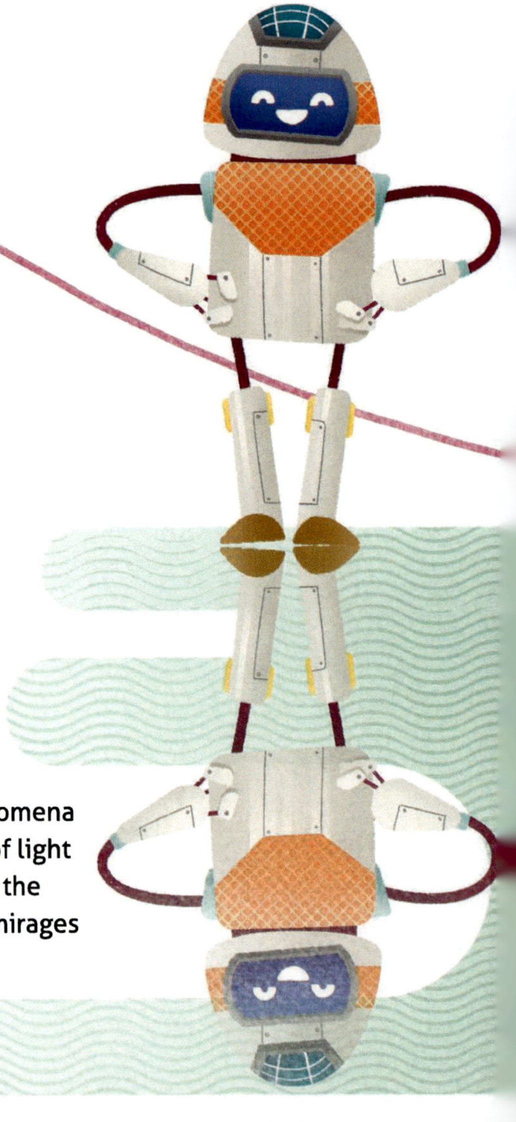

PERCEPTUAL

These are caused by the visual system; for example, images that don't actually exist, or ambiguous forms.

COGNITIVE

These are caused by the brain's interpretation of images. A typical example is impossible figures.

People were already familiar with illusions in antiquity. Greeks and Romans used them to decorate their homes, and two important ancient authors, **Aristotle** and **Lucretius**, spoke of them in their works.

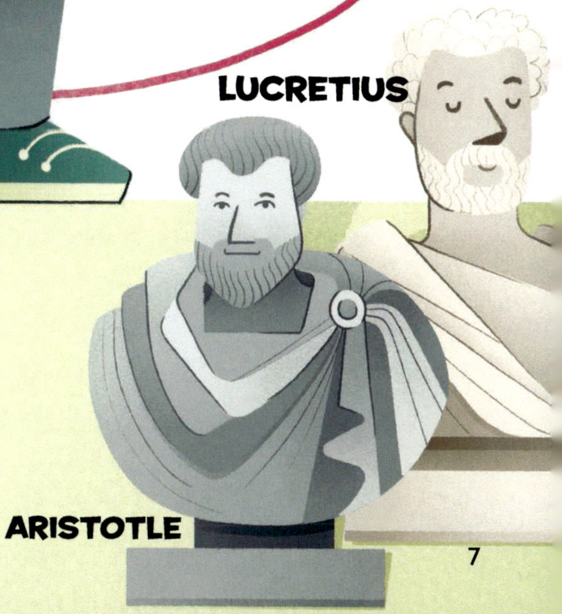

ESCHER'S ROOM

Impossible objects can only exist on paper because they are absolutely impossible. The artist **MAURITS CORNELIS ESCHER** was an expert in creating impossible objects.

ESCHER was a big fan of OPTICAL ILLUSIONS, and he was able to create truly impossible universes. His works not only deceive our brain, but also hide mathematical and geometric formulas.

LOOK CLOSELY!
HOW MANY
IMPOSSIBLE
OBJECTS CAN YOU
SEE IN THIS ROOM?

IMPOSSIBLE OBJECTS (SOLUTIONS)

Parts are in front of and behind each other at the same time.
(WINDOW)

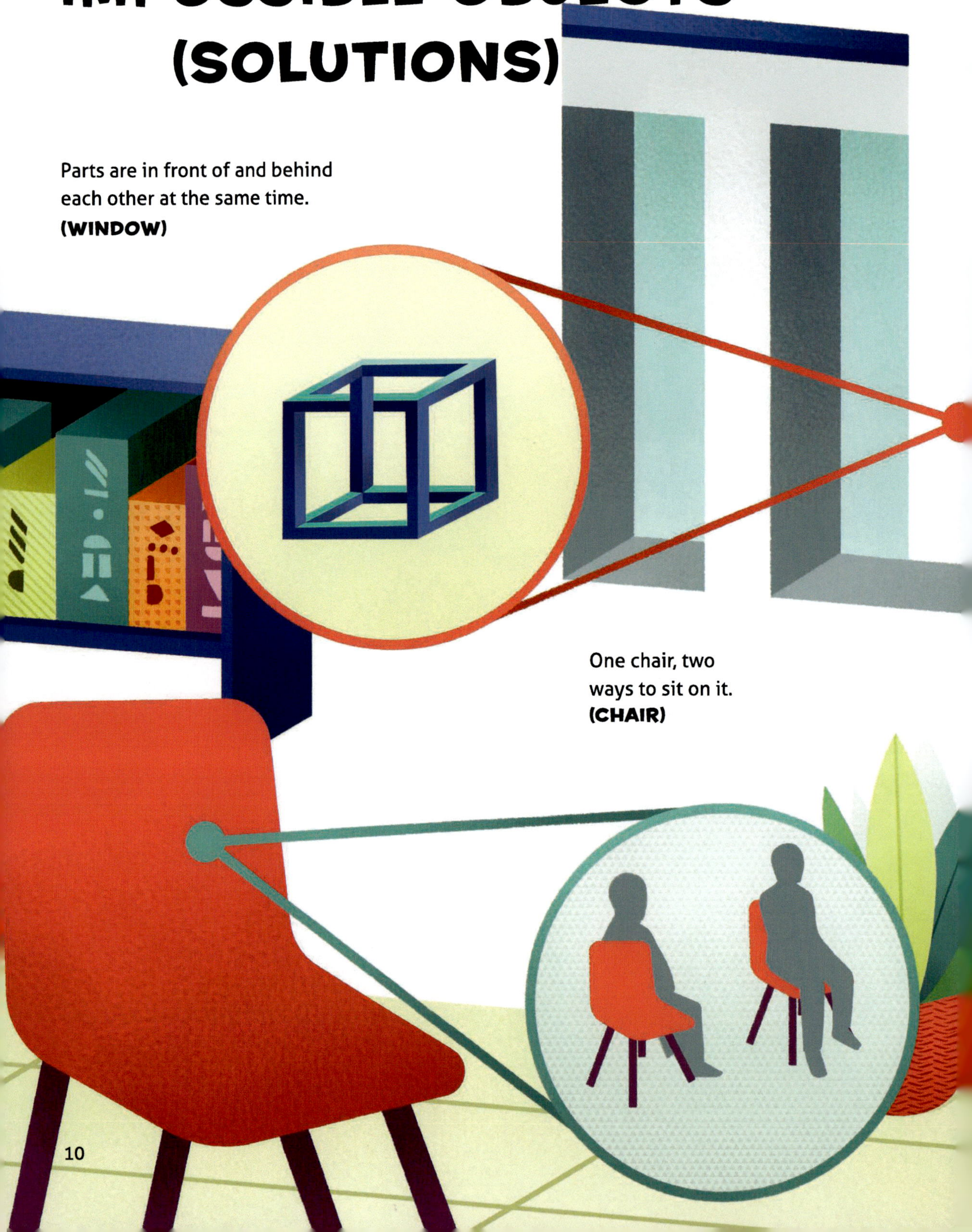

One chair, two ways to sit on it.
(CHAIR)

The top viewed from above and the bottom viewed from below.
(LAMP)

Two legs at the bottom, with a recess at the top.
(TABLE)

TEST THE TEXT

READ THE TEXT IN THE BOXES QUICKLY.

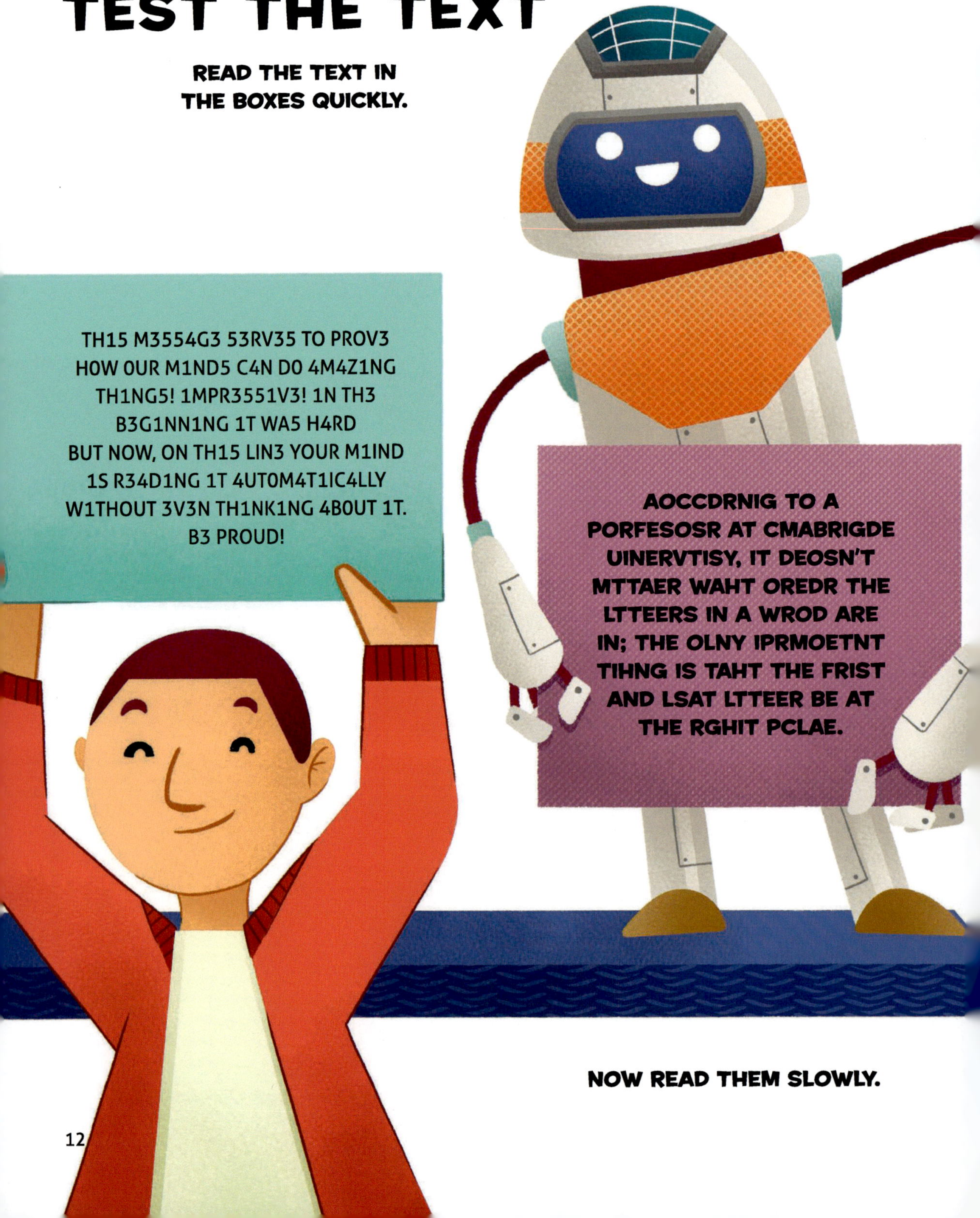

TH15 M3554G3 53RV35 TO PROV3 HOW OUR M1ND5 C4N DO 4M4Z1NG TH1NG5! 1MPR3551V3! 1N TH3 B3G1NN1NG 1T WA5 H4RD BUT NOW, ON TH15 LIN3 YOUR M1IND 1S R34D1NG 1T 4UTOM4T1IC4LLY W1THOUT 3V3N TH1NK1NG 4BOUT 1T. B3 PROUD!

AOCCDRNIG TO A PORFESOSR AT CMABRIGDE UINERVTISY, IT DEOSN'T MTTAER WAHT OREDR THE LTTEERS IN A WROD ARE IN; THE OLNY IPRMOETNT TIHNG IS TAHT THE FRIST AND LSAT LTTEER BE AT THE RGHIT PCLAE.

NOW READ THEM SLOWLY.

Our brains process an enormous amount of information. Over time, the brain has learned to use strategies to speed up some learning processes in order not to become overloaded, trying to grasp the essence and therefore automatically completing general information.

OPTICAL ART

Isn't this amazing? It's called **OPTICAL ART**, and it's a very common type of art, born in the US in the 1960s.

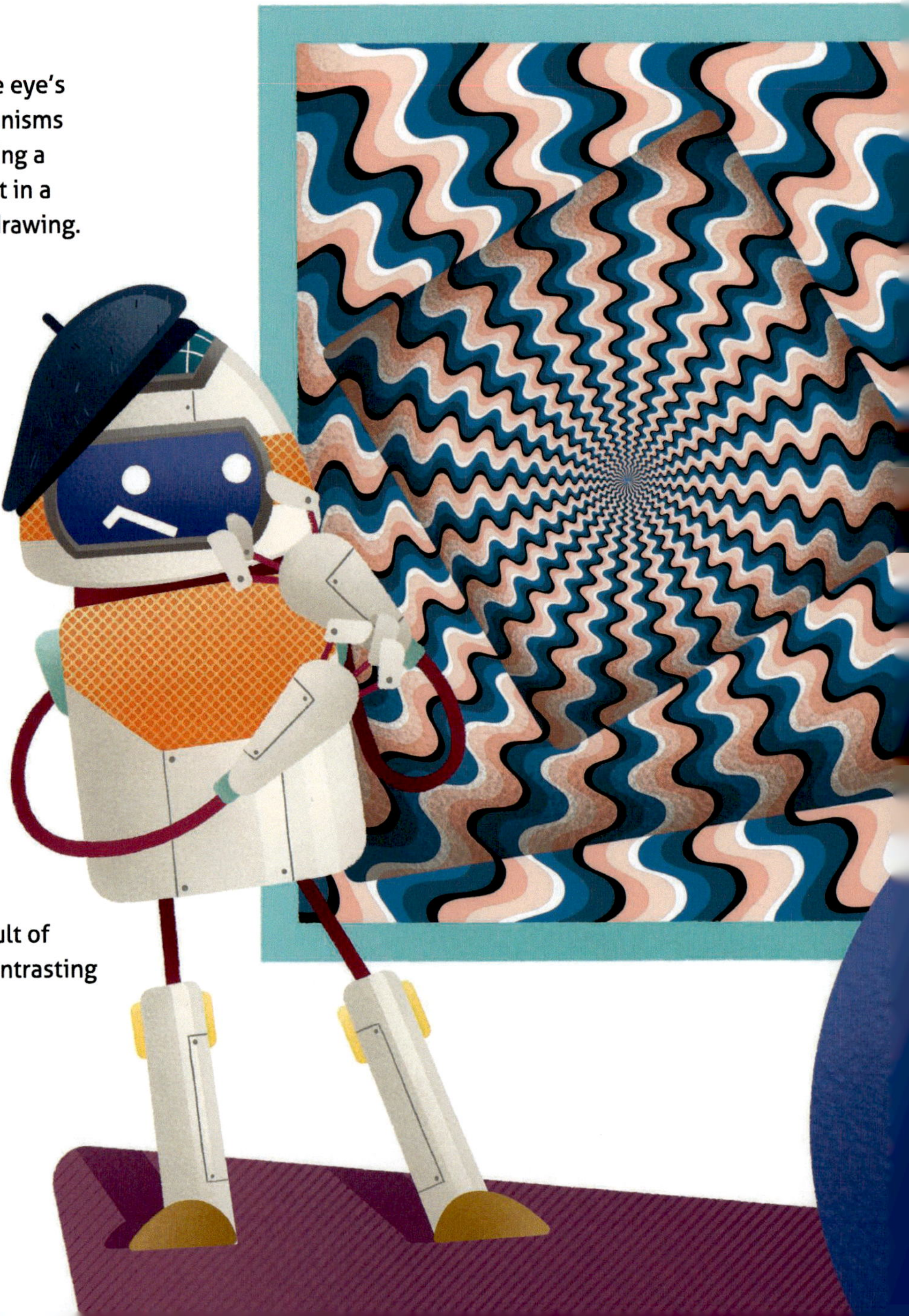

Optical art uses the eye's own control mechanisms to deceive it, creating a sense of movement in a completely static drawing.

The effect is the result of the interaction of contrasting colors and shapes.

SCIENCE AND ART

Some of the artists who do these works are expert researchers and neuroscientists; that's because it is essential to understand the VISUAL SYSTEM if you want to deceive the eyes and brain, and create the illusion of movement.

Science is still unable to fully explain how all these phenomena occur.

THEY'RE THERE, BUT NOT REALLY

This is the **Hermann grid**! It is named after **LUDIMAR HERMANN**, who described the illusion in 1870. When you look at the whole grid, you can see gray spots at the intersections of the white bars... but they're not really there!

The difference between the two illusions is that the second one already has white spots in the intersections, while there are no spots at all in the intersections of the Hermann grid.

In 1994, Bernd Lingelbach and Michael Schrauf came up with the scintillating grid illusion. When you look at it, you will see black spots appearing and disappearing over the white ones, but the black spots are not real.

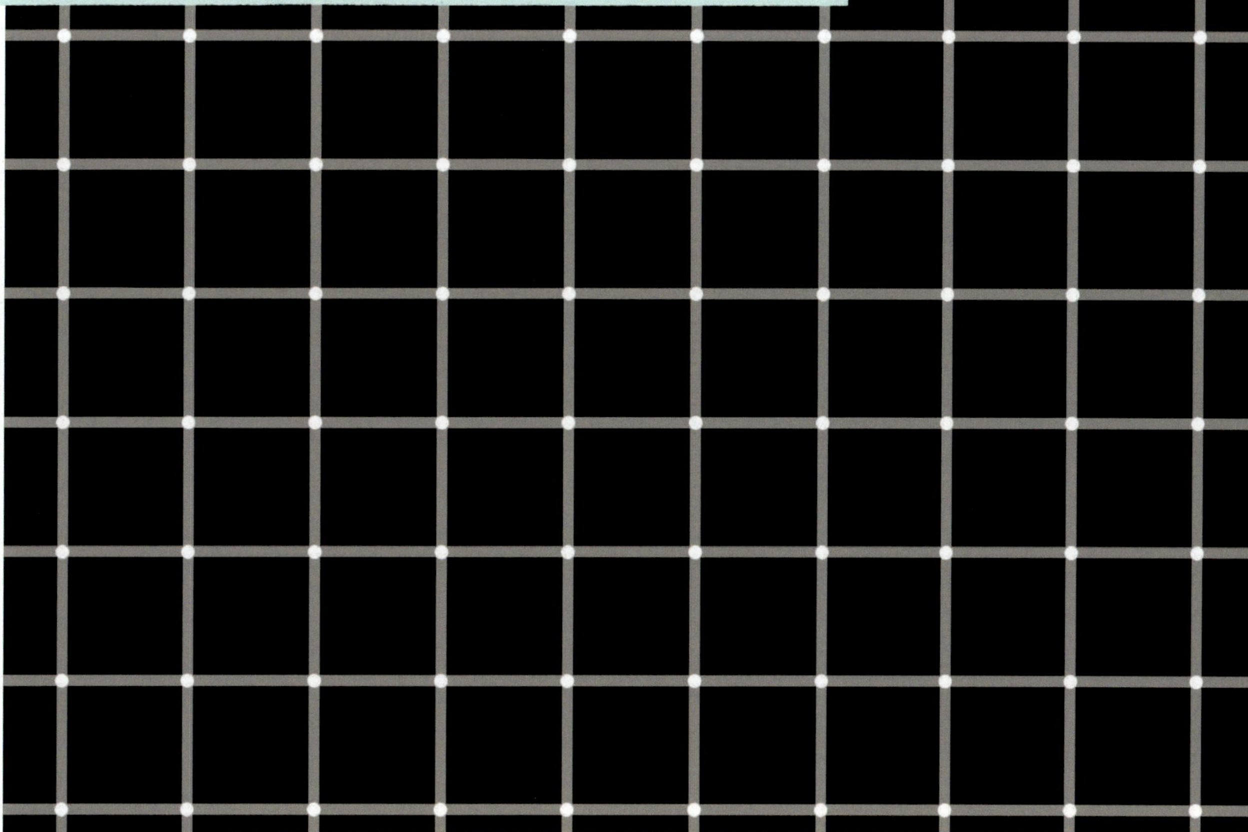

It is believed that these OPTICAL ILLUSIONS are caused by the different light intensity in the various areas of the grid and by the way our eyes send some signals to the brain while blocking others. It appears that this mechanism helps the brain identify object boundaries better and simultaneously distinguish between light and dark images.

THE KANIZSA TRIANGLE

This illusion was first described in 1955, by the Italian psychologist **GAETANO KANIZSA.**

In the picture, you can see two superimposed equilateral white triangles, but the triangle on top has not actually been drawn with lines. Also, the white triangle without an outline appears brighter than the other one.

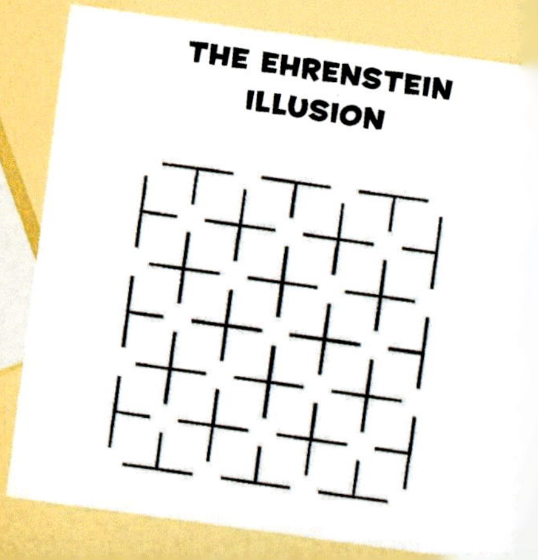

Other examples are **Idesawa's spiky sphere** and the **Ehrenstein illusion.**

HOW TO DO IT

DIFFICULTY:

DIRTINESS:

TIME: *15 minutes*

DO IT WITH:

YOU WILL NEED

- *a ruler*
- *a compass*
- *a pencil*
- *a black marker*

1

Start with the Kanizsa triangle and recreate the same illusion.

2

Now, try doing the same thing with a square.

3

Draw 4 black circles, each without one quarter; arrange the four missing quarters at 90°, so that a white square appears in the middle.

4

Now, try and recreate the other illusions on the previous page!

WHAT HAPPENS

If you have been precise, thanks to this COGNITIVE ILLUSION you will see a white square appear in the middle of your drawing.

WORDS THAT AREN'T THERE

What word can you see in this image?

You are looking at a word that isn't there.

It is created by the shadows of imagined white letters on a white background.

* FLY

YOU WILL NEED

- *a pencil*
- *2 sheets of paper*

HOW TO DO IT

DIFFICULTY: 3 out of 5

DIRTINESS: 1 out of 5

TIME: *20 minutes*

DO IT WITH: –

1

On the first sheet of paper, write the word ILLUSION.

2

Now cover it with the second sheet of paper.

3

Hold the sheets of paper against a window and look carefully at the outline of the letters, imagining that they are three-dimensional.

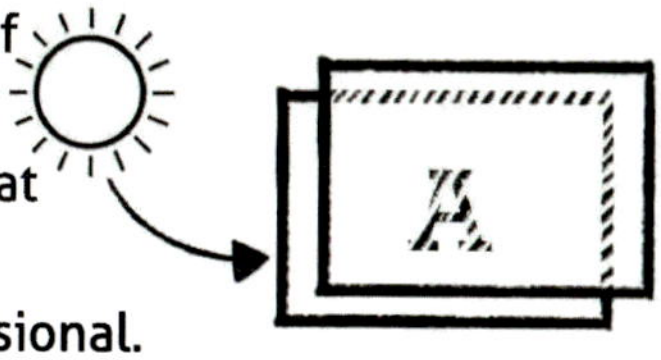

4

Draw the imaginary shadows, as if the letters were illuminated from the top left-hand corner of the sheet of paper.

5

Now show someone the sheet of paper with just the shadows and ask them what's written on it.

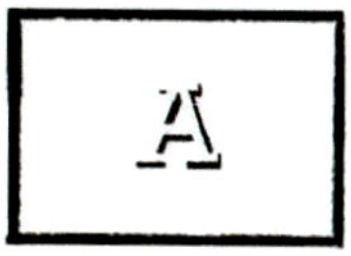

WHAT HAPPENS

You have recreated the effect! The word isn't there, but people can still read it by only looking at the shadows.

AMBIGRAMS!

AMBIGRAMS first appeared in the 19th century, but these strange word designs weren't given a name until 1980, when **Scott Kim** called them **inversions**.

AMBIGRAMS, or inversions, are calligraphic designs that can be read as two or more different words. They have rotational symmetry, so the words read the same when they are inverted.

The term **AMBIGRAM** was coined by philosopher **DOUGLAS HOFSTADTER** in 1986, and he made it famous with his book *Ambigrams: An Ideal Microworld for the Study of Creativity*.

A famous AMBIGRAM appears in **Dan Brown**'s book *Angels and Demons*, as well as in the film of the same name by director **Ron Howard**.

AMBIGUOUS FIGURES

These are images that can be **interpreted differently** because they show **two distinct figures**. You may be able to see both figures immediately or only after someone else points out the second one.

Above, is this the profile of a man playing the saxophone? Or is it a woman's face? To the left, if you had to choose a railing for your balcony, which one would you choose: black or white?

DRAW AN AMBIGUOUS FIGURE

YOU WILL NEED
- *a pencil*
- *2 sheets of 8.5" x 11" paper*
- *scissors*
- *a black marker*

DIFFICULTY: 2 of 5

DIRTINESS: 1 of 5

TIME: *10 minutes*

DO IT WITH: –

HOW TO DO IT

1. Look carefully at the vase at the top of the opposite page and take note of the details that make it possible to also see two faces in profile.

2. Fold a sheet of paper in half so that you can draw on one half.

3. Now draw the profile of half a vase while at the same time trying to make it look like a face in profile.

4. Cut out the profile of the vase, cutting through both halves of the paper, then open the sheet of paper.

5. Color the vase with the black marker and put it onto the other sheet of white paper.

WHAT HAPPENS

You have created an ambiguous figure inspired by ***Rubin's vase:*** *It can either be seen as a vase or as two faces. The brain first interprets the image in one way, then in another. It cannot perceive the vase and the faces simultaneously.*

PAREIDOLIA

PAREIDOLIA is our mind's tendency to recognize familiar objects in otherwise random or unrelated objects or patterns. How many times have you stopped to look at a cloud and tried to find the shape of an animal or the features of a face?

THE MARTIAN FACE

A famous example of PAREIDOLIA is the "face"on Mars. This Martian rock formation was captured by the Viking 1 space probe, and it resembles a human face when the light hits the rock at a certain angle.

PAREIDOLIA AND VEGETABLES

In the 16th century, the artist **GIUSEPPE ARCIMBOLDO** was already using PAREIDOLIA to create bizarre portraits. At a quick glance, we can see "human" faces, but we soon start noticing that the details are created with fruit, vegetables, flowers, and other objects.

THE IMPORTANCE OF CONTEXT

The black circle in the image on the right looks bigger than the one on the left, but both are the same size. This illusion occurs because the brain uses context to determine the size of objects.

Since the circle on the right is surrounded by smaller circles, the brain believes that it is bigger than the circle surrounded by larger ones. This is called the **Ebbinghaus illusion!**

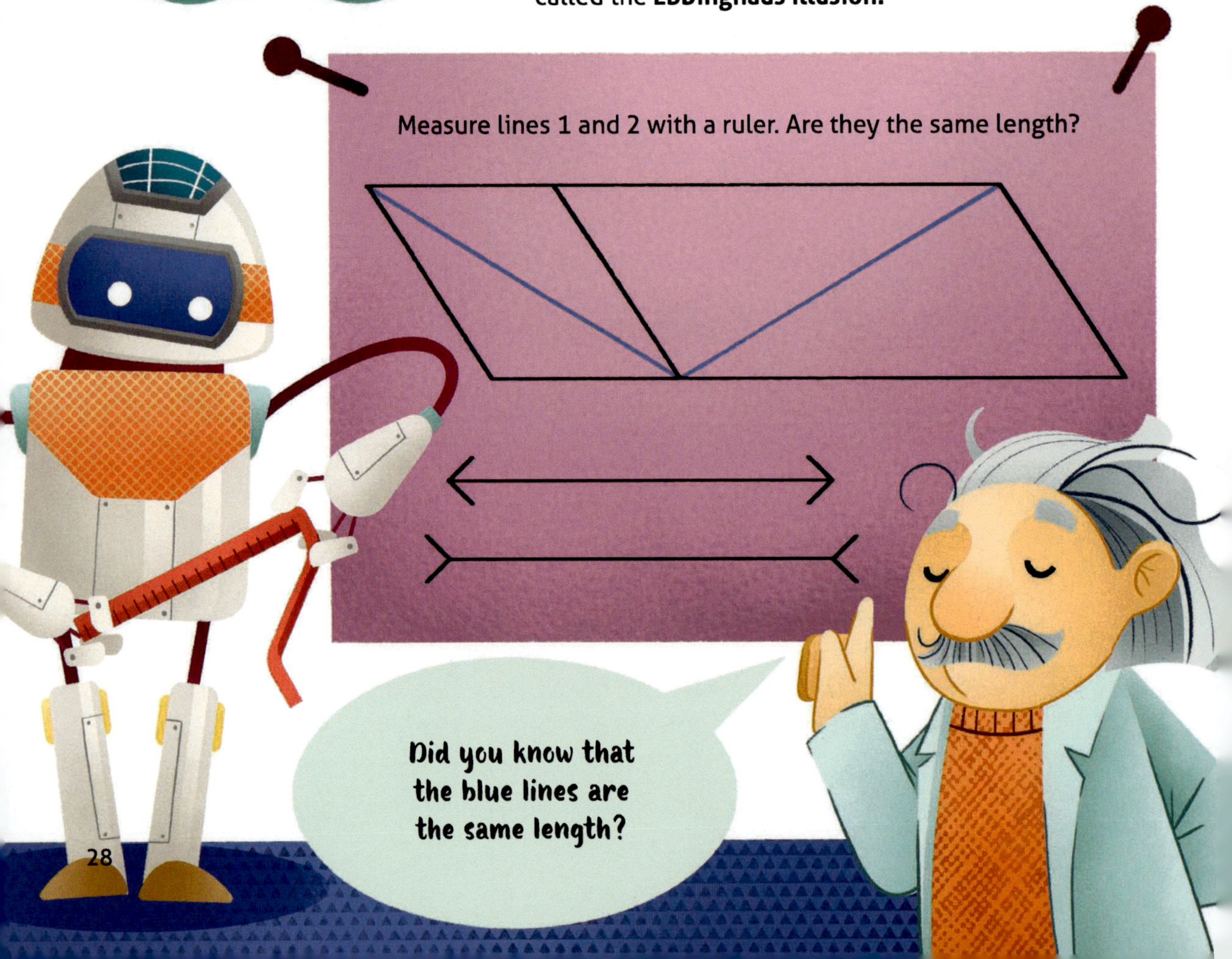

YOU WILL NEED

- *a compass*
- *scissors*
- *2 pieces of different colored card stock*
- *a pencil*

DIFFICULTY: 2/5

DIRTINESS: 2/5

TIME: *30 minutes*

DO IT WITH: –

HOW TO DO IT

1 Draw two circles with a diameter of 2.5 inch (6.3 cm) on one of the pieces of card stock.

2 Cut out the two circles.

3 Draw six 8-inch (20 cm) circles and eight 1-inch (2.5 cm) circles on the other sheet of card stock.

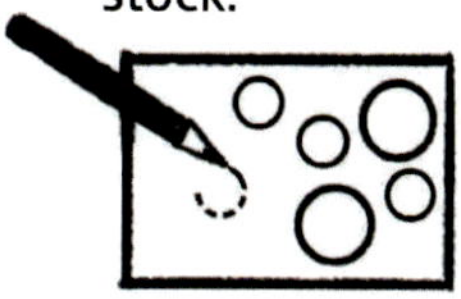

4 Cut out all the circles.

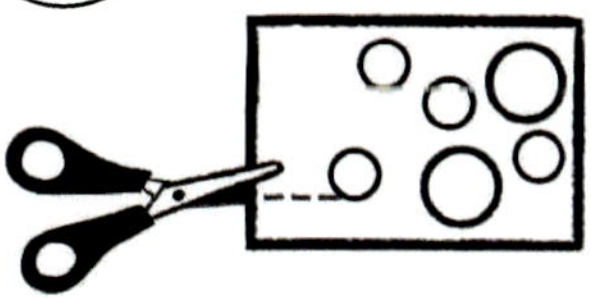

5 Arrange the circles in the same way as those in the Ebbinghaus illusion on the facing page.

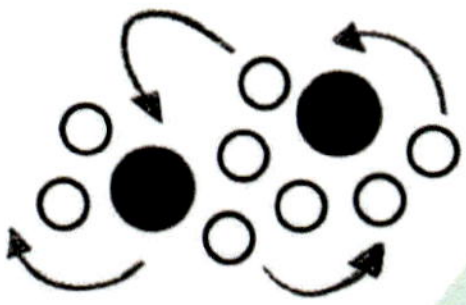

WHAT HAPPENS

Once you have created the illusion on the table, you will see how difficult it is to believe that the first two circles are the same size, even though you made them yourself!

THE CAFÉ WALL ILLUSION

RICHARD GREGORY discovered this illusion, called the café wall illusion, in a bar in the 1970s. The straight lines look slanted, but they are actually parallel.

The lines that separate the white squares appear slanted because the brain struggles to perceive them as being parallel. This effect is due to the strong contrast between black and white and the fact that the squares are not in straight lines.

The black and white tiles that Gregory observed in the café were staggered and not set out like a perfect checkerboard, and therefore the grout lines between the tiles didn't look as if they were parallel.

YOU WILL NEED

- *a sheet of white card stock measuring 15 x 11 in (38.5 X 27.5 cm)*
- *a black marker*
- *a ruler*
- *scissors*

DIFFICULTY:

DIRTINESS:

TIME: *20 minutes*

DO IT WITH:

HOW TO DO IT

1

Draw 5 lines on the card stock, 2 in (5.5 cm) apart.

2

Now draw 7 columns, 2 in (5.5 cm) apart.

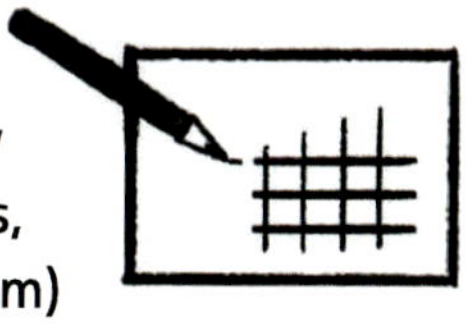

3

Color every other square black to create a checkerboard.

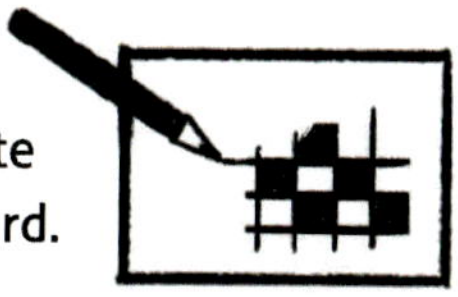

4

Cut out the rows of squares.

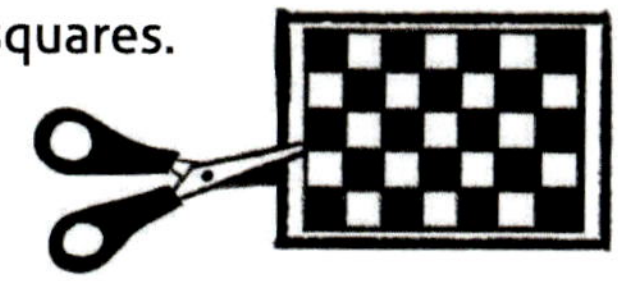

5

Move every other row half a square to the right.

WHAT HAPPENS

You will notice that the dividing lines appear to converge, whereas they are actually still parallel. If you reassemble the checkerboard as you drew it, the dividing lines will once again look parallel.

A THREE-SIDED CUBE

A cube is a three-dimensional shape with six sides, but a drawing of a cube only shows three of them.

DIFFICULTY:

DIRTINESS:

TIME: *15 minutes*

DO IT WITH: -

YOU WILL NEED

- *a sheet of white card stock*
- *a ruler*
- *a pencil*
- *scissors*
- *Scotch tape*

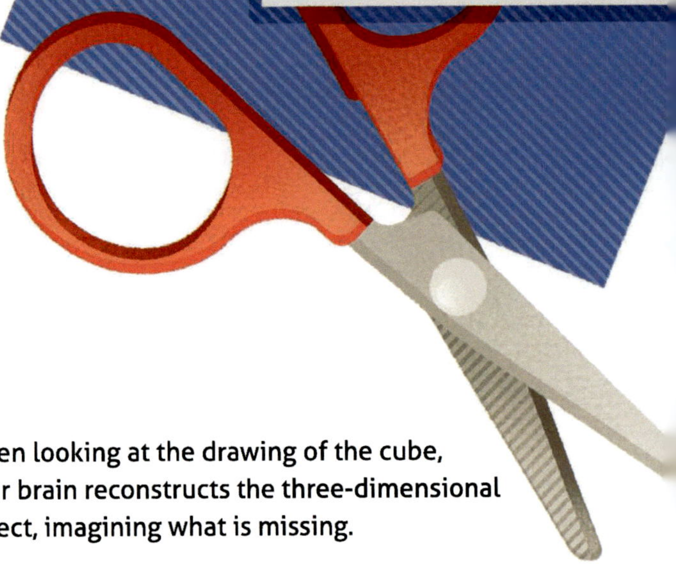

When looking at the drawing of the cube, your brain reconstructs the three-dimensional object, imagining what is missing.

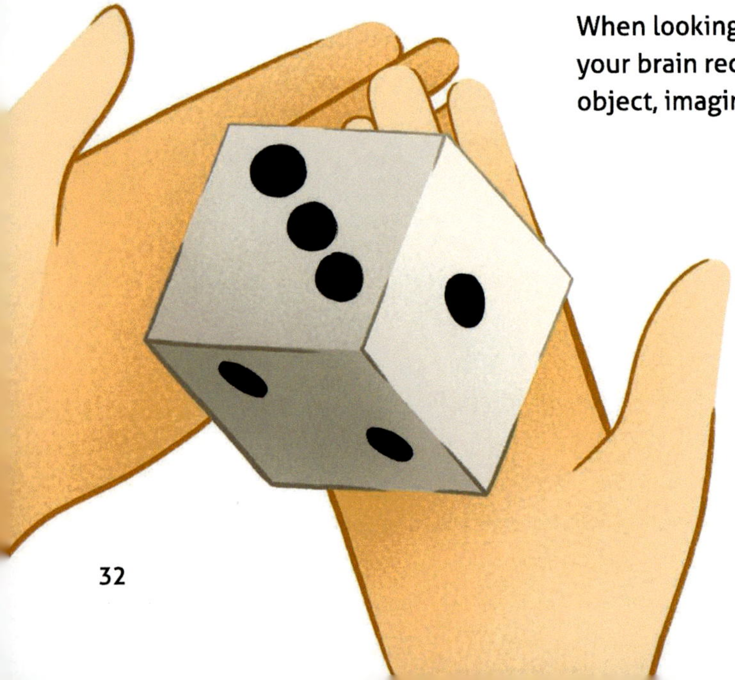

We can mislead our brain by showing it a concave object that it will actually perceive as a convex cube.

HOW TO DO IT

1. On the card stock, draw three squares with 4 in (10 cm) sides, as shown in the illustration.

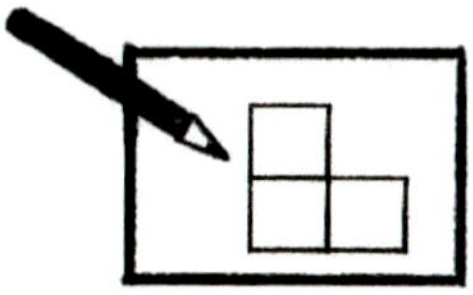

2. Cut along the outside line of the figure, to obtain a large L shape.

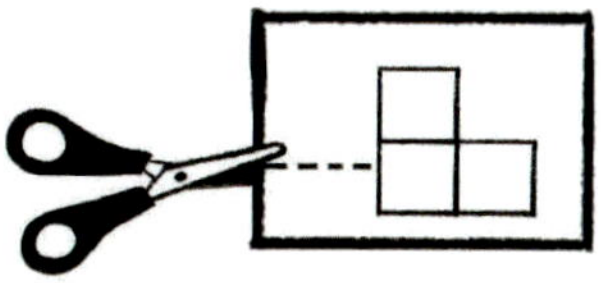

3. Draw one dot in the middle of the first square, two dots on the second, and three dots in a diagonal line on the third.

4. Fold along the lines highlighted in the illustration so that the dots are on the outside of the object.

5. Stick the sides together at the back using Scotch tape.

6. Move the object and look at it with one eye.

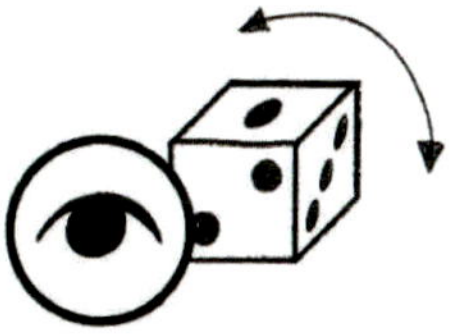

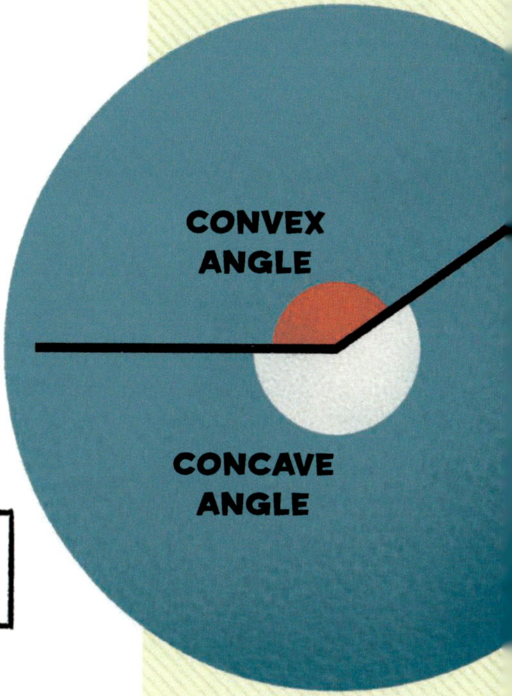

WHAT HAPPENS

You will have the sensation of seeing a normal convex die, but it will look as if it is moving in the opposite direction to what it actually is.

THE PENROSE TRIANGLE

DISCOVERED TWICE!

This illusion was first discovered by **Oscar Reutersvärd**, a Swedish graphic artist. A famous anecdote says that he drew it at the age of 18 while doodling during a Latin lesson at school.

OSCAR REUTERSVÄRD

The illusion was also later discovered independently by **LIONEL SHARPLES PENROSE** and his son **ROGER PENROSE**, both famous scientists and philosophers.

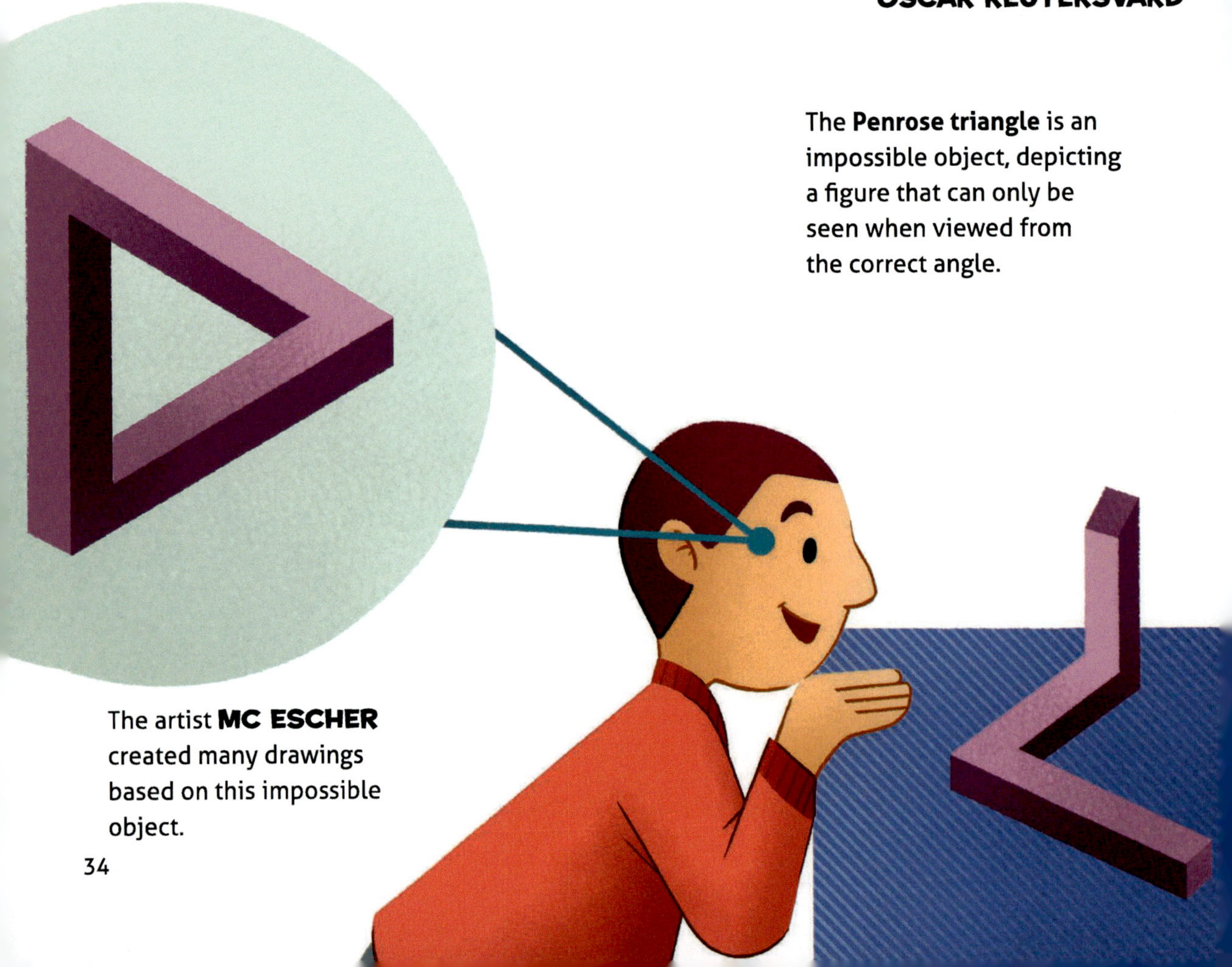

The **Penrose triangle** is an impossible object, depicting a figure that can only be seen when viewed from the correct angle.

The artist **MC ESCHER** created many drawings based on this impossible object.

HOW TO DO IT

YOU WILL NEED
- *12 in (30 cm) of iron wire*
- *pliers*

DIFFICULTY:

DIRTINESS:

TIME: *15 minutes*

DO IT WITH:

+

1

Create a U shape with the wire, with each section being 4 in (10 cm) long, making two 90° angles.

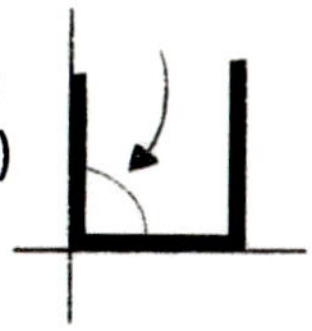

2

Holding the wire U between your thumb and forefinger, bend the right side down 90°.

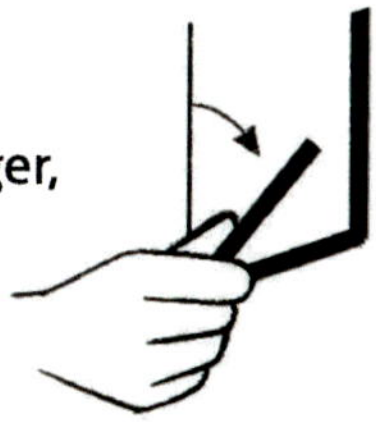

3

Hold the middle section of the iron wire with your right hand.

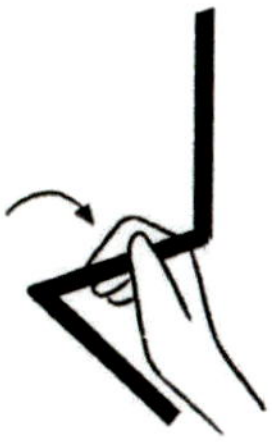

4

Close your left eye and look at the object with your right eye.

5

Now tilt the middle section 45° to the left and try to see the two outer sections joined together to form the last corner of the triangle.

WHAT HAPPENS

The triangle can only be seen when viewed from the correct angle. In a three-dimensional space, this object cannot exist, but thanks to an illusion we are able to see it.

FREEHAND LINES

DIFFICULTY:

DIRTINESS:

TIME: *15 minutes*

DO IT WITH:

YOU WILL NEED

- *a pencil*
- *an eraser*
- *colored markers*
- *a sheet of paper*

You can recreate the illusion of three-dimensional thickness with simple lines drawn on a sheet of paper.

HOW TO DO IT

1 Put your hand in the middle of the sheet of paper.

2 Draw around your hand with a pencil.

WARNING!

Be precise when joining the lines at the edges of the hand with the arched lines. The more lines you draw, the better the end result will be.

3 Take your hand off the paper.

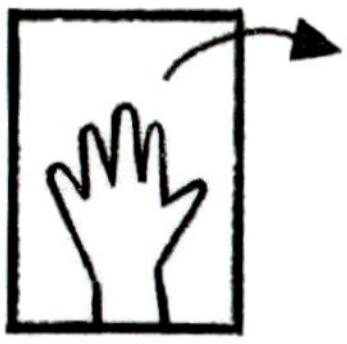

4 Using a black marker, draw parallel lines across the sheet of paper. They should be straight until you get to the pencil outline. Once inside the outline of your hand, arch the lines upward, then make them straight again on the other side of the outline.

5 Erase the pencil lines.

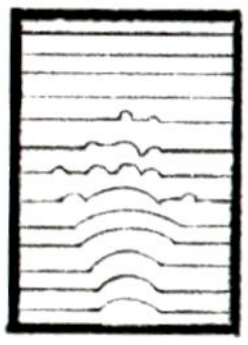

6 Color the spaces inside the black lines with different colors

WHAT HAPPENS

When the drawing is complete, your hand will appear in 3D.

PHÉNAKI... WHAT?

The **phénakisticope** is an object that makes it possible to perceive a sequence of drawings as **animated images**.

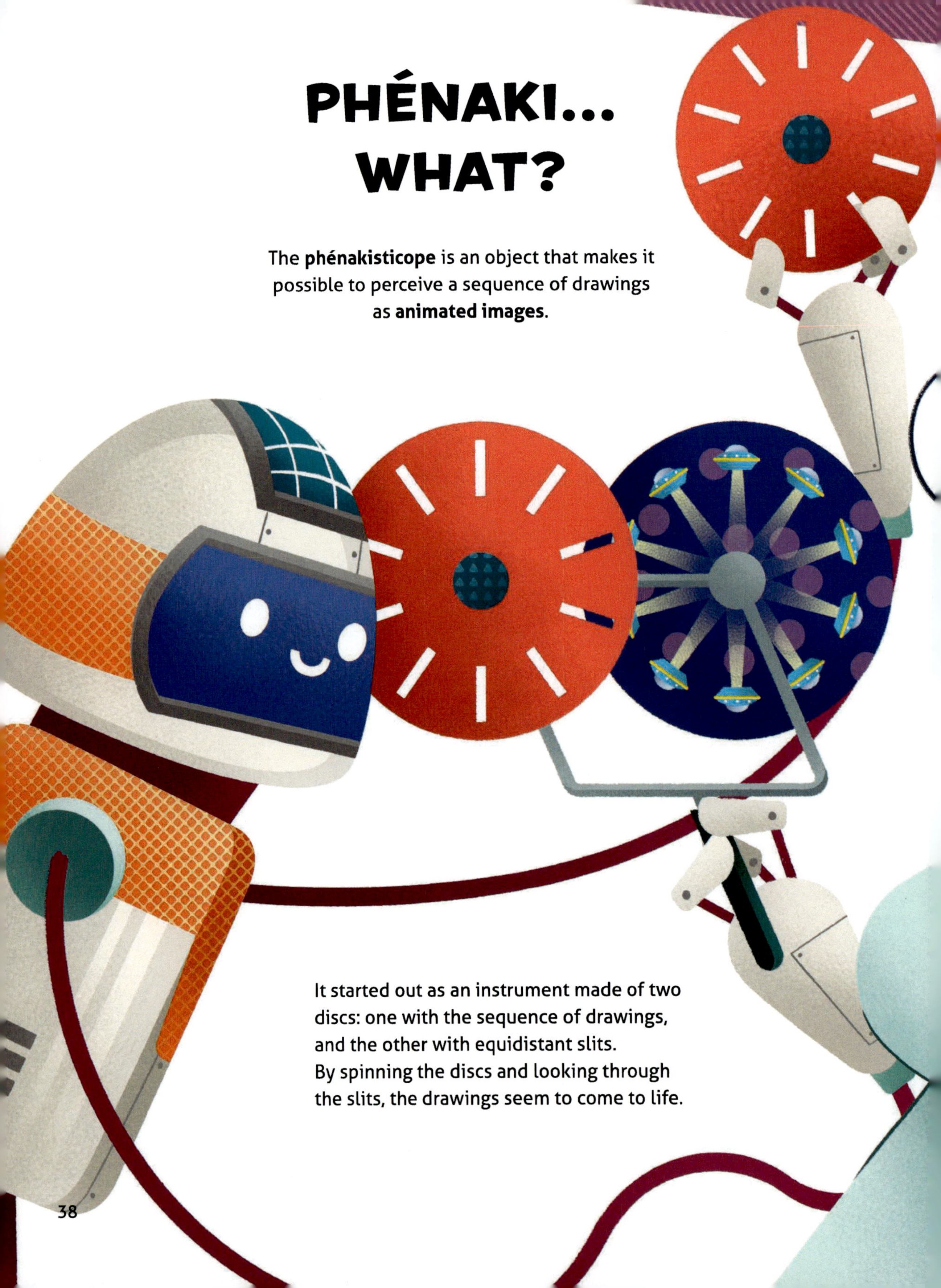

It started out as an instrument made of two discs: one with the sequence of drawings, and the other with equidistant slits. By spinning the discs and looking through the slits, the drawings seem to come to life.

There is also a version consisting of one disc with slits and images. You hold the disc in front of a mirror and look through the slits. When you spin the disc, the images come to life in the mirror.

The term "phénakisticope" comes from a Greek word that means "to deceive," which is exactly what happens since the cleverly drawn objects appear to move.

IN THE 19TH CENTURY...

DIFFICULTY:

DIRTINESS:

TIME: *50 minutes*

DO IT WITH:

+

YOU WILL NEED

- *a circle of white card stock with a diameter of 8 in (20 cm)*
- *a pencil*
- *a ruler*
- *a utility knife*
- *a thumbtack*

HOW TO DO IT

1

Divide the circle into 16 equal segments by drawing 8 lines.

2

Draw a circle in the first segment. In the next segment, draw another circle but a little higher than the first. Continue like this until you get to the ninth segment, where you start drawing the circles a little lower than the previous one. The last circle should be the same height as the first one.

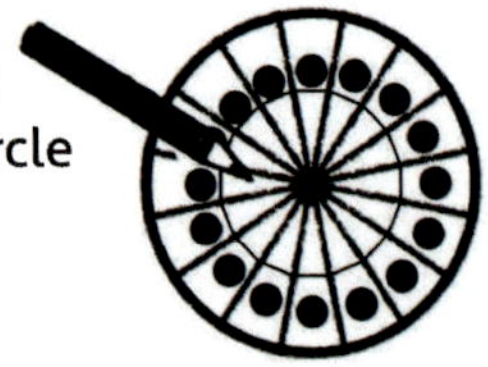

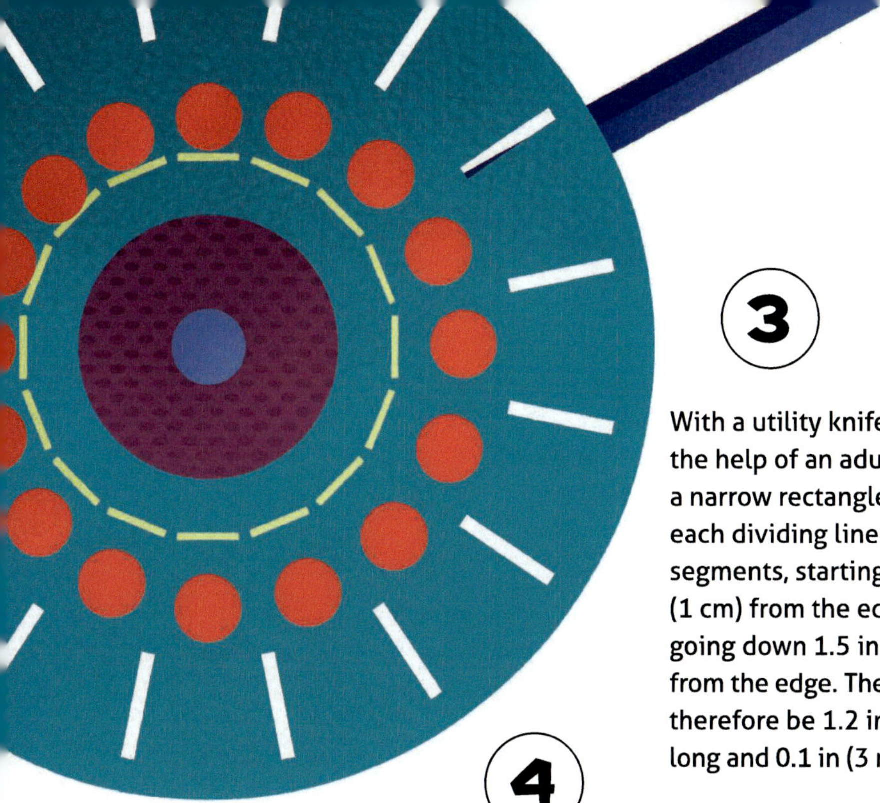

3

With a utility knife and the help of an adult, remove a narrow rectangle from each dividing line of the segments, starting 0.4 in (1 cm) from the edge and going down 1.5 in (4 cm) from the edge. The slit must therefore be 1.2 in (3 cm) long and 0.1 in (3 mm) wide.

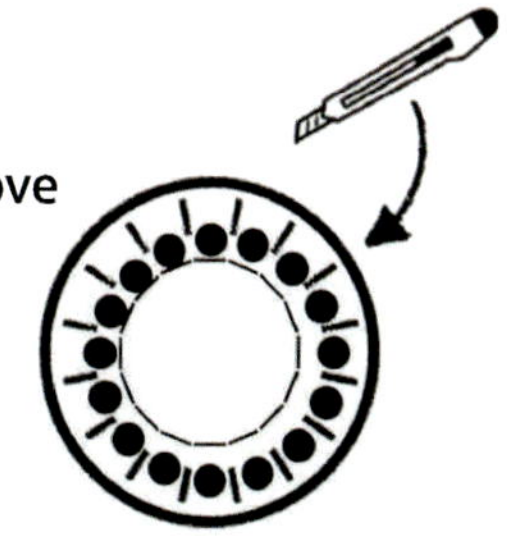

4

Attach the disc to the top of the pencil with the thumbtack.

5

Stand in front of a mirror and face the drawings toward the mirror.

6

Spin the disc in front of your eyes and watch the reflection of the drawings through the slits.

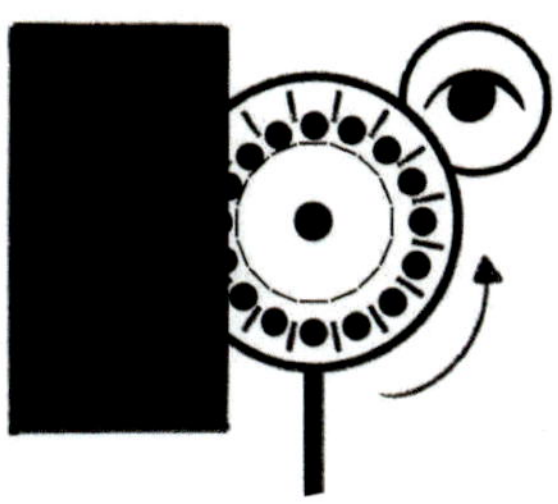

WHAT HAPPENS

We have the sensation of seeing an animated image of a ball bouncing on the ground. This is due to PERSISTENCE OF VISION, a characteristic of our VISUAL SYSTEM that cannot distinguish two images if one is replaced too quickly by another.

MOVING IMAGES

The **zoetrope** is an OPTICAL device that produces the illusion of images in motion. It was invented by **WILLIAM GEORGE HORNER** in 1833 and was very popular in the Victorian era.

It consists of a sequence of drawings on a strip of paper, which is placed inside a cylinder with slits in it, through which you watch the images.

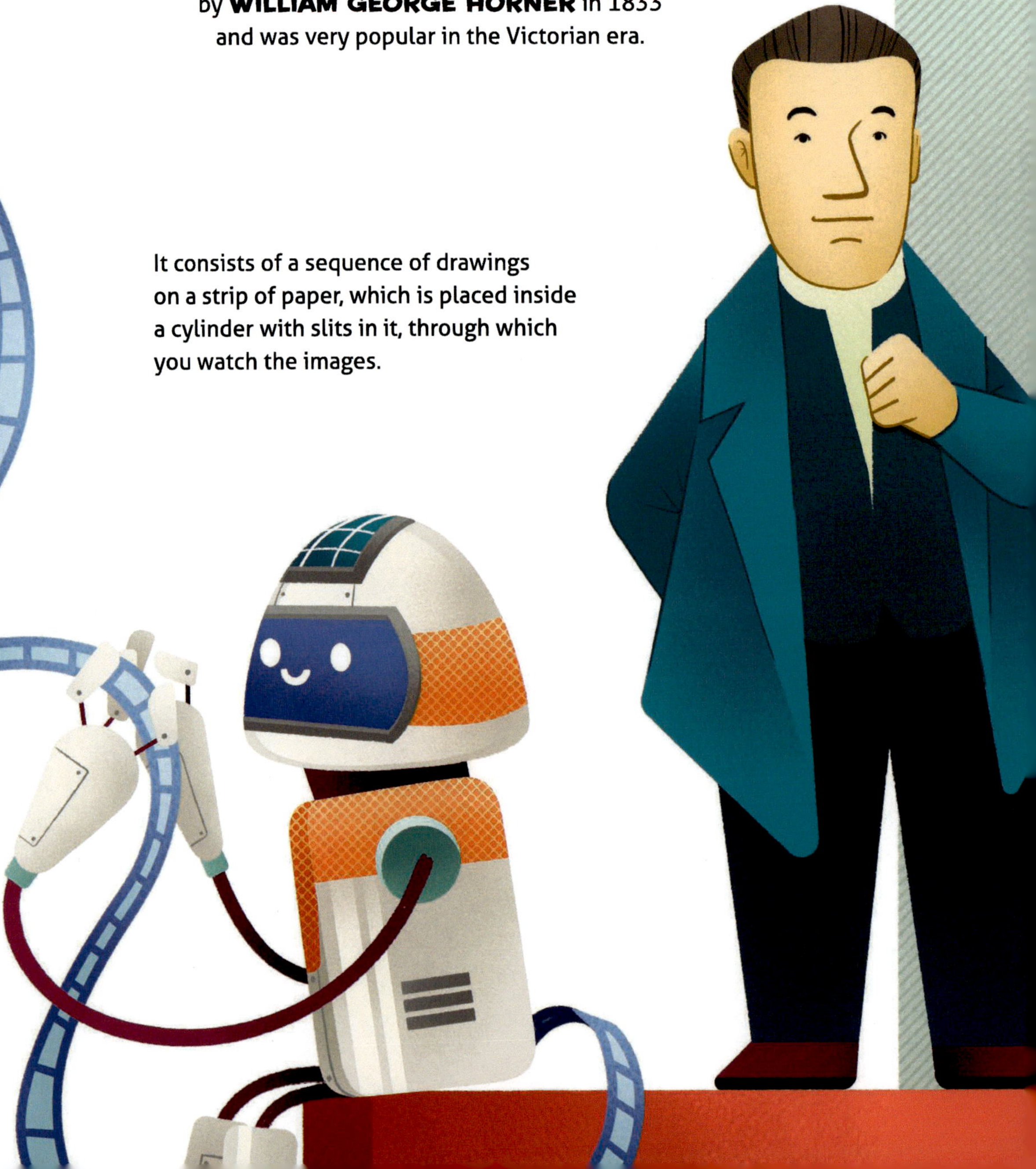

When making one, it is important that the slits are regularly spaced and that there are the same number of slits as drawings (there must be one slit for each drawing in the sequence).

The zoetrope and the phénakisticope are precursors of film, which was invented in the late 1800s. On December 28, 1895, brothers **LOUIS AND AUGUSTE LUMIÈRE** held the world's first public movie screening.

THE ZOETROPE

DIFFICULTY:

DIRTINESS:

TIME: *50 minutes*

DO IT WITH: +

YOU WILL NEED

- *a cylindrical plastic container, about 4 in (10 cm) high, with a diameter of about 6 in (15 cm)*
- *a nail*
- *a round wooden board, 8 in (20 cm) in diameter and 0.8 in (2 cm) thick*
- *a utility knife*
- *a black permanent marker*
- *a strip of paper 2 in (5 cm) wide and as long as the circumference of the container*
- *a pencil*
- *a washer*

HOW TO DO IT

1. Draw a sequence of 16 drawings on the strip of paper, like those for the phénakisticope, all the same size and equidistant from each other.

2. Color the jar black.

3. Glue the strip of paper with the drawings onto the inside of the container, with the drawings facing inward.

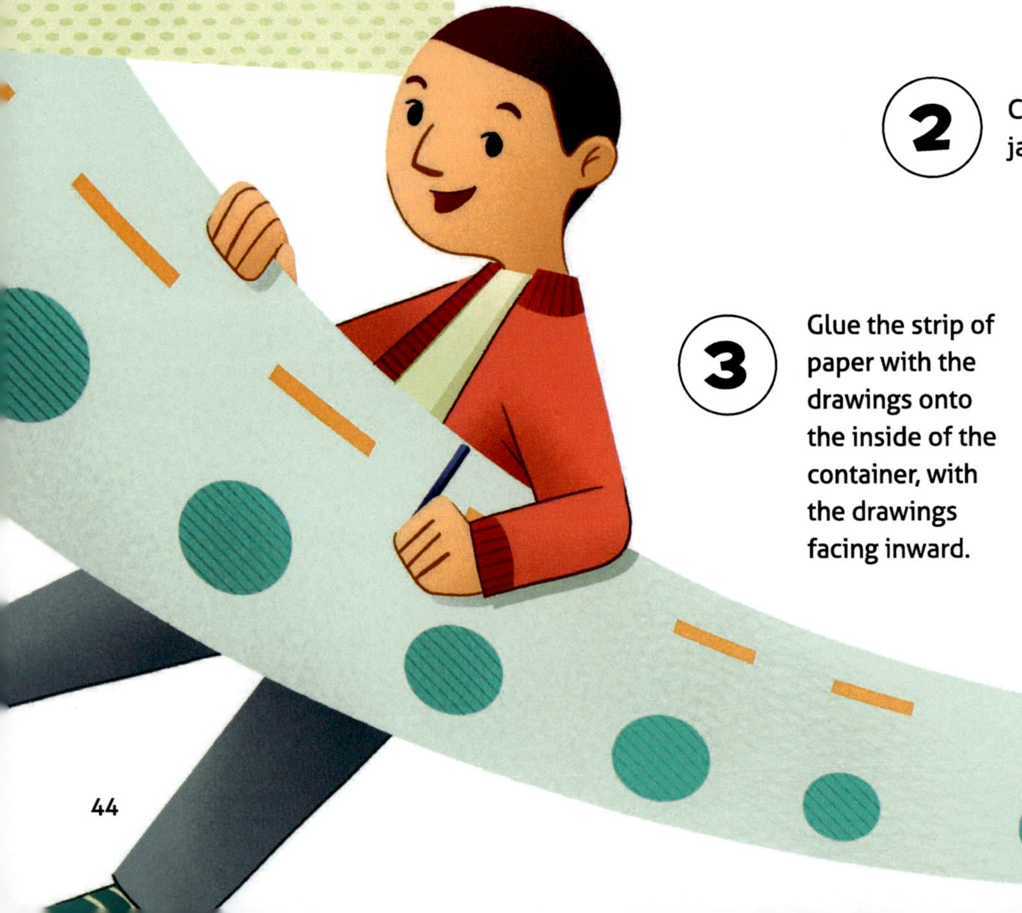

4 With the help of an adult, use the utility knife to cut sixteen 3-mm-wide slits in the container, exactly above each space between one drawing and the next.

5 Attach the bottom of the container to the wooden board with the nail, inserting the washer between them so the container can spin freely.

6 Lift the container to eye level and look through the slits. Spin the container and watch the drawings inside.

WHAT HAPPENS

As with the phénakisticope, your PERSISTENCE OF VISION makes it seem as if the sequence of drawings comes to life.

MORE

Make more strips of paper of the same size and create more series of drawings.

GLOSSARY

AMBIGRAMS: These are calligraphic designs that can be read as two or more different words. By turning them around, it is possible to read the different words they are composed of.

COGNITIVE ILLUSION: An illusion where our visual system deceives us due to the brain's interpretation of images. Impossible figures are an example.

ESCHER, MAURITS CORNELIS (1898–1972): A Dutch artist whose work combines art and science, challenging perception and our sense of logic by creating impossible universes that hide mathematical formulas and optical illusions.

GREGORY, RICHARD (1923–2010): A British psychologist and professor of neuropsychology at the University of Bristol who is famous for the café wall illusion, which he discovered in 1973 when looking at the wall tiles of a café in Bristol, England.

HERMANN, LUDIMAR (1838–1914): A German physician who, in 1870, discovered the Hermann grid illusion (named after him), while reading a physics text. The phenomenon was actually also observed in 1844 by Sir David Brewster, a Scottish scientist and the inventor of the kaleidoscope.

HOFSTADTER, DOUGLAS RICHARD (1945–): An American scholar of the mind and its processes. In 1986, he invented the term "ambigram."

HORNER, WILLIAM GEORGE (1786–1837): A British mathematician who, in 1834, invented the zoetrope, also known as the wheel of life, to create the illusion of moving images. He is also remembered for Horner's rule, a method for solving algebraic equations.

KANIZSA, GAETANO (1913–1993): An Italian psychologist from Trieste who is famous for having described, in 1955, the illusion of the Kanizsa triangle, which is now found in books about visual perception across the world.

OPTICAL: This describes the area of science that studies light. In particular, it explores its behavior, properties, and interaction with matter.

OPTICAL ART (OP ART): This is a type of abstract art; that is, it does not depict reality. It was developed in the US around 1960 by artists experimenting with the optical illusion of movement through geometric shapes, colors, and light in order to involve the observer.

OPTICAL ILLUSION: An illusion where our visual system deceives us due to phenomena related to the physical properties of light. Example: desert mirages.

PAREIDOLIA: This is our mind's tendency to recognize familiar objects in otherwise random or unrelated objects or patterns. Example: when we see objects or faces in clouds.

PENROSE, LIONEL SHARPLES (1898–1972) AND ROGER (1931–): British father and son, one a biologist and the other a mathematician, physicist, and cosmologist, who published and popularized the illusion that bears their name: the Penrose triangle.

PERCEPTUAL ILLUSION: An illusion where our visual system deceives us due to the way our eyes have developed and how they function.

PERSISTENCE OF VISION: When images that reach the retina (a membrane at the back of the eye that captures information and then sends it to the brain) remain etched in our visual system for a certain amount of time. Even if it is only a short time, it prevents you from seeing new images.

VISUAL SYSTEM: Our visual system includes both the eyes, which collect information, and the brain, which interprets the information and then revises it.

VALERIA BARATTINI

Valeria holds a master's degree in Economics and Management of Arts and Cultural Activities from the University of Ca 'Foscari in Venice and a master's in Standards for Museum Education from the Roma Tre University. She works in education and cultural planning. Since 2015, she has been working in partnership with Fosforo, holding events and activities in the field of scientific dissemination and informal teaching.

MATTIA CRIVELLINI

A graduate of Computer Science at the University of Bologna, Mattia has been studying Cognitive Sciences in the United States at Indiana University. Since 2011, he has been the director of Fosforo, the science festival of Senigallia. He organizes and plans activities, conferences, and shows for communication and dissemination of science in Italy and abroad through the NEXT Cultural Association.

ALESSANDRO GNUCCI

Alessandro is a science communicator and tutor with over 15 years of experience. In 2011, he founded Fosforo, the science festival in Senigallia, and in 2014, he founded the NEXT Cultural Association. He designs science communication formats and organizes shows with his colleagues at the PSIQUADRO association.

ROSSELLA TRIONFETTI

After graduating in Applied Arts, Rossella specialized in the field of illustration and graphics, attending various courses with professionals in the sector, including at the Mimaster of Milan. Currently, she works as an illustrator of children's books and also collaborates in the creation of apps. In recent years, she has illustrated several books for White Star Kids.

Valeria, Mattia, Alessandro, and Rossella are all part of

FOSFORO: THE SCIENCE FESTIVAL.

Fosforo: It's a fair, a festival, a meeting place. It's a series of events to give stimuli, overturn the commonplace, make people fall in love with science, and stimulate them to dream, think, invent, and discover. *Fosforo*: It's scientific dissemination. An event with national and international guests who animate Senigallia, in the Marche region of Italy, for 4 days in May. This is done with surprising scientific exhibitions, laboratories, and conferences on the main scientific topics.

Published in 2023
by The Rosen Publishing Group, Inc.
29 East 21st Street, New York, NY 10010

Cataloging-in-Publication Data

Names: Names: Crivellini, Mattia, author. | Trionfetti, Rossella, illustrator.
Title: Optical illusions / by Mattia Crivellini, illustrated by Rossella Trionfetti.
Description: New York : PowerKids Press, 2023. |
Series: Let's experiment | Includes glossary.
Identifiers: ISBN 9781725339347 (pbk.) |
ISBN 9781725339354 (library bound) |
ISBN 9781725339361 (ebook)
Subjects: LCSH: Optical illusions--Experiments--Juvenile literature.
Classification: LCC QP495.B378 2023 |
DDC 152.14'8--dc23

Manufactured in the United States of America

CPSIA Compliance Information: Batch #CSPK23. For further information contact Rosen Publishing, New York, New York at 1-800-237-9932.

Find us on